AF504393

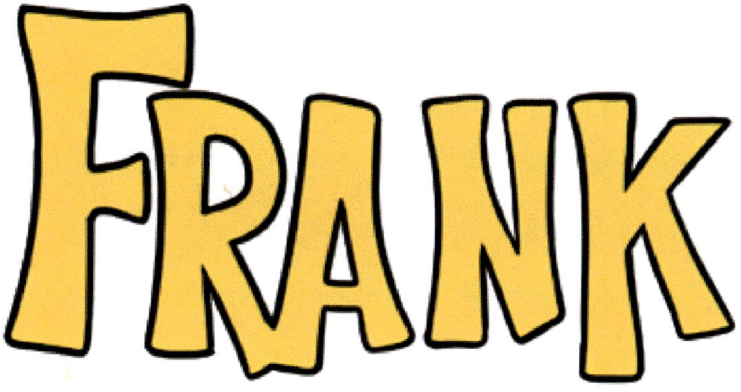

James P. Bernard

Dedication

This book is dedicated to my family. They have given and continue to give me the strength, love and support I needed to complete this dream.

Acknowledgment

I would like to acknowledge, my wife, Kristen, for her editorial help as well as her keen insight into the illustrations that were finally developed and chosen for this book. Her ability to see things I missed was a valuable part of the process that created "Frank".

Of course I would be remiss if I did not give special thanks to our children and grandchildren who listened to me telling Frank stories when they were growing up. Their love and patience were inspirational.

In addition, I must credit my parents for the help they gave me while I was growing up. Their love, trust and guidance made me the man I am today. Without that support, I could not have written this book.

And finally to my late father-in-law, Richard Dube, many thanks for the hours of putting up with my shenanigans in his kind and patient way. He grounded us all.

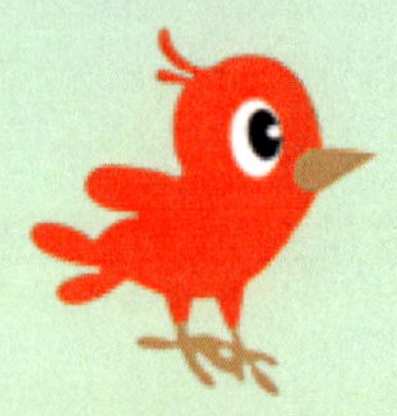

Frank was a small being with a gigantic heart. He also had special powers that would allow him to grow bigger or become very tiny, depending on what he thought was best. In fact, he could become anything he wanted to be. All he had to do was to think very hard about what he wanted to be and suddenly, that was what he would become.

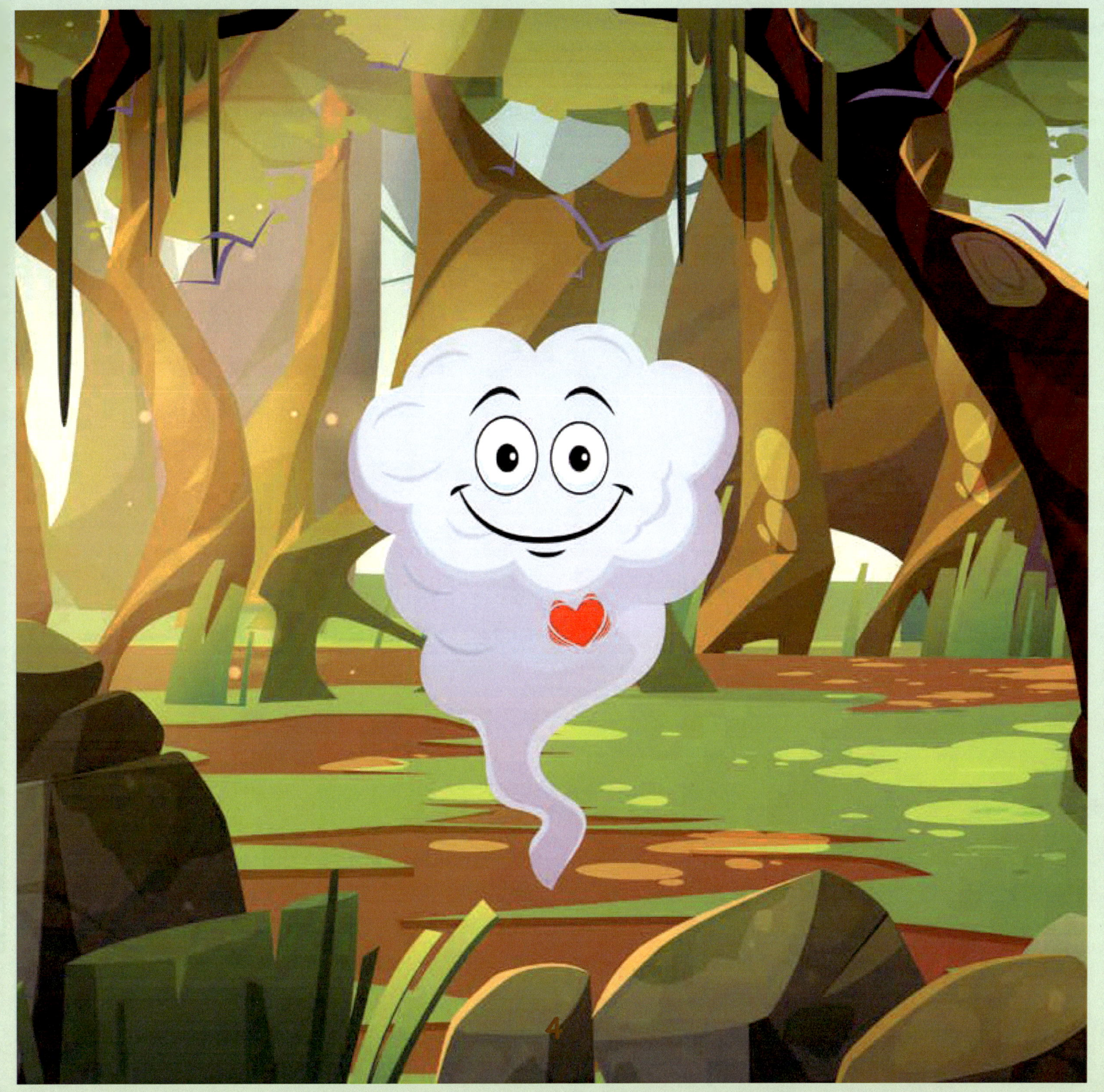

He lived alone in the woods. He thought that was best because he did not want to scare anyone or anything. You see, Frank did not look like you or me or anyone for that matter, and that could be very scary to almost everyone.

The problem was that Frank's huge heart was always ready to help people, animals or even plants if they were in trouble or needed help.

But because he was different, people were afraid of him and as a result, he had no friends and was lonely. He only wanted to help whenever possible.

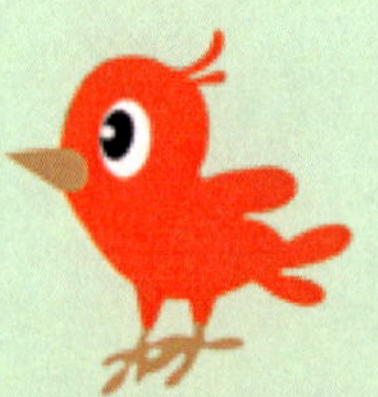

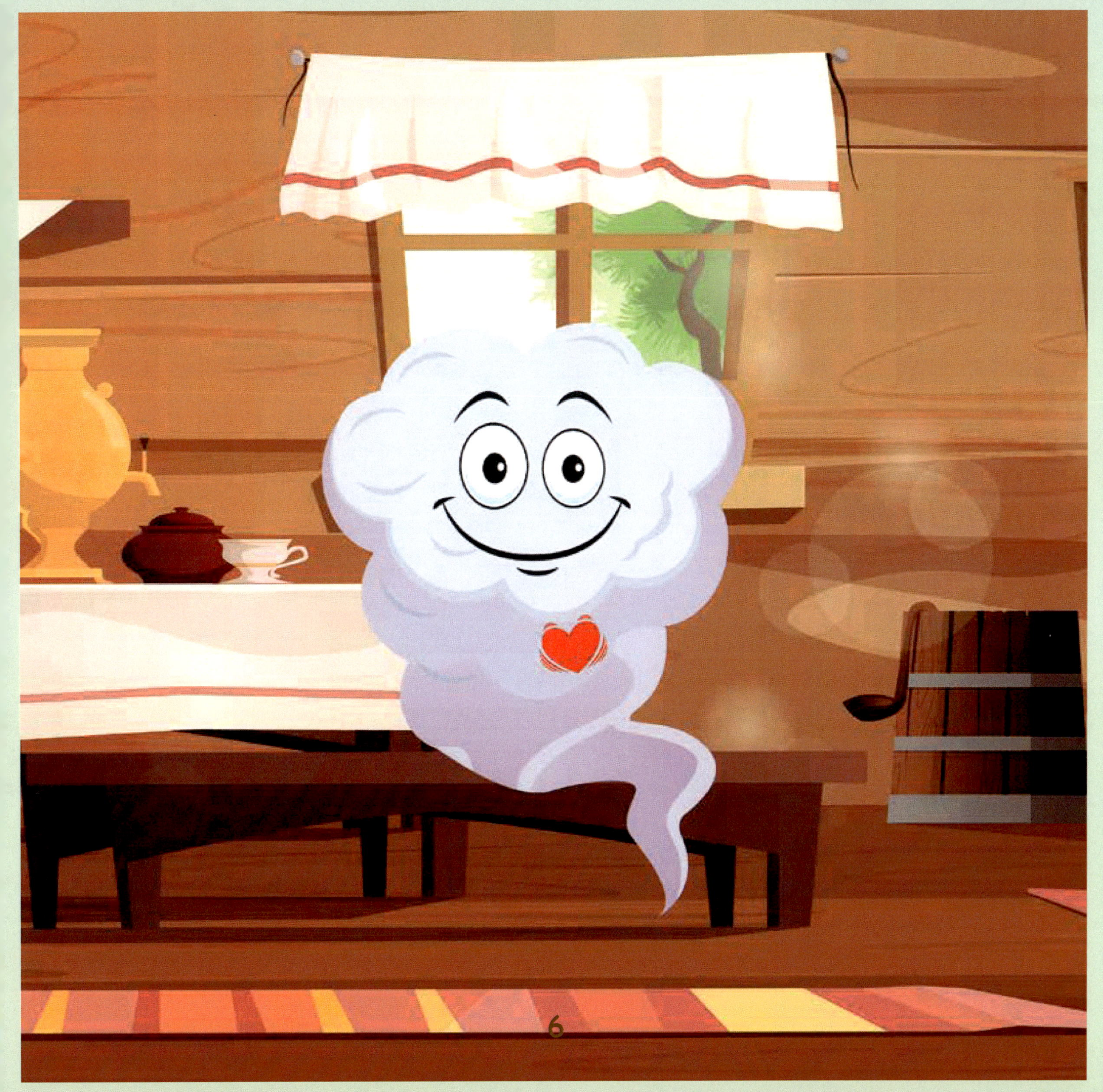

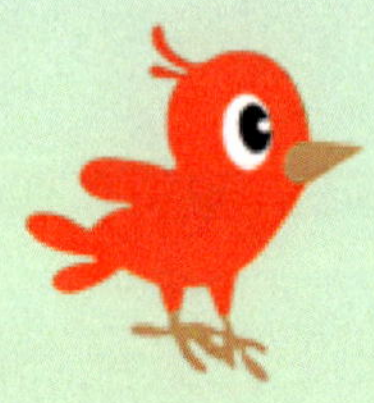

One day, Frank was moving through the woods when he heard what he thought was crying. At first, he was shocked and did not believe what he heard, because no one ever came into the woods.

They knew that something lived in the woods, and they were afraid.

Frank looked all around the woods until he heard the crying sound getting closer to him.

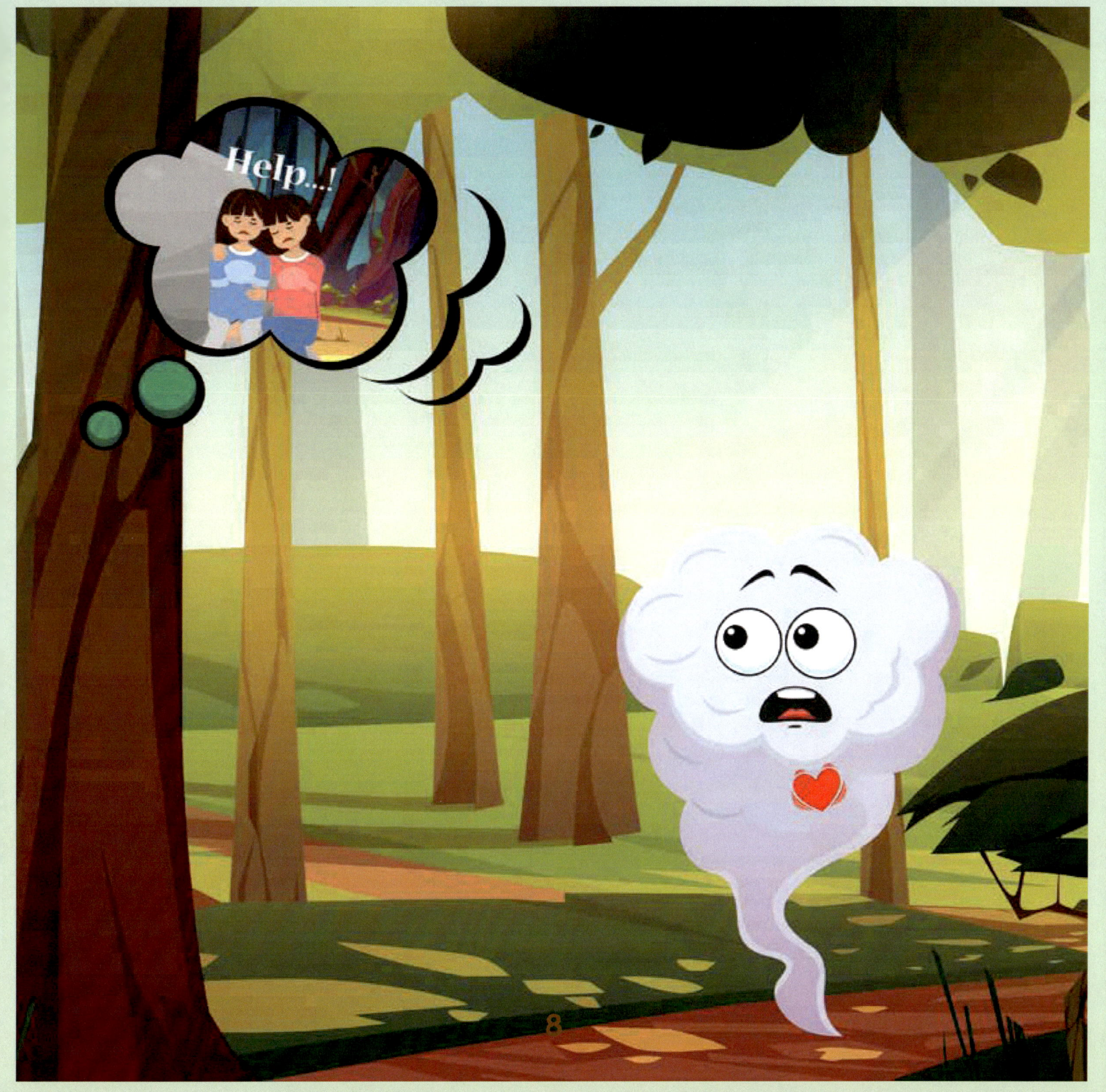

Help...!

He peeked around a big rock and there, holding on to each other, were two little girls. They were whimpering. Frank thought they must have been lost and scared.

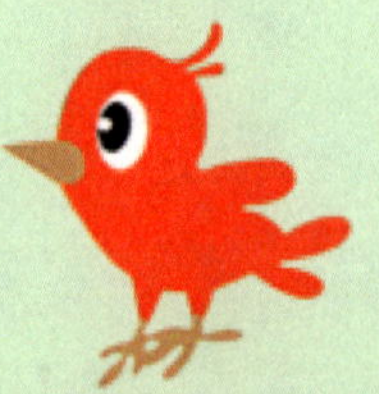

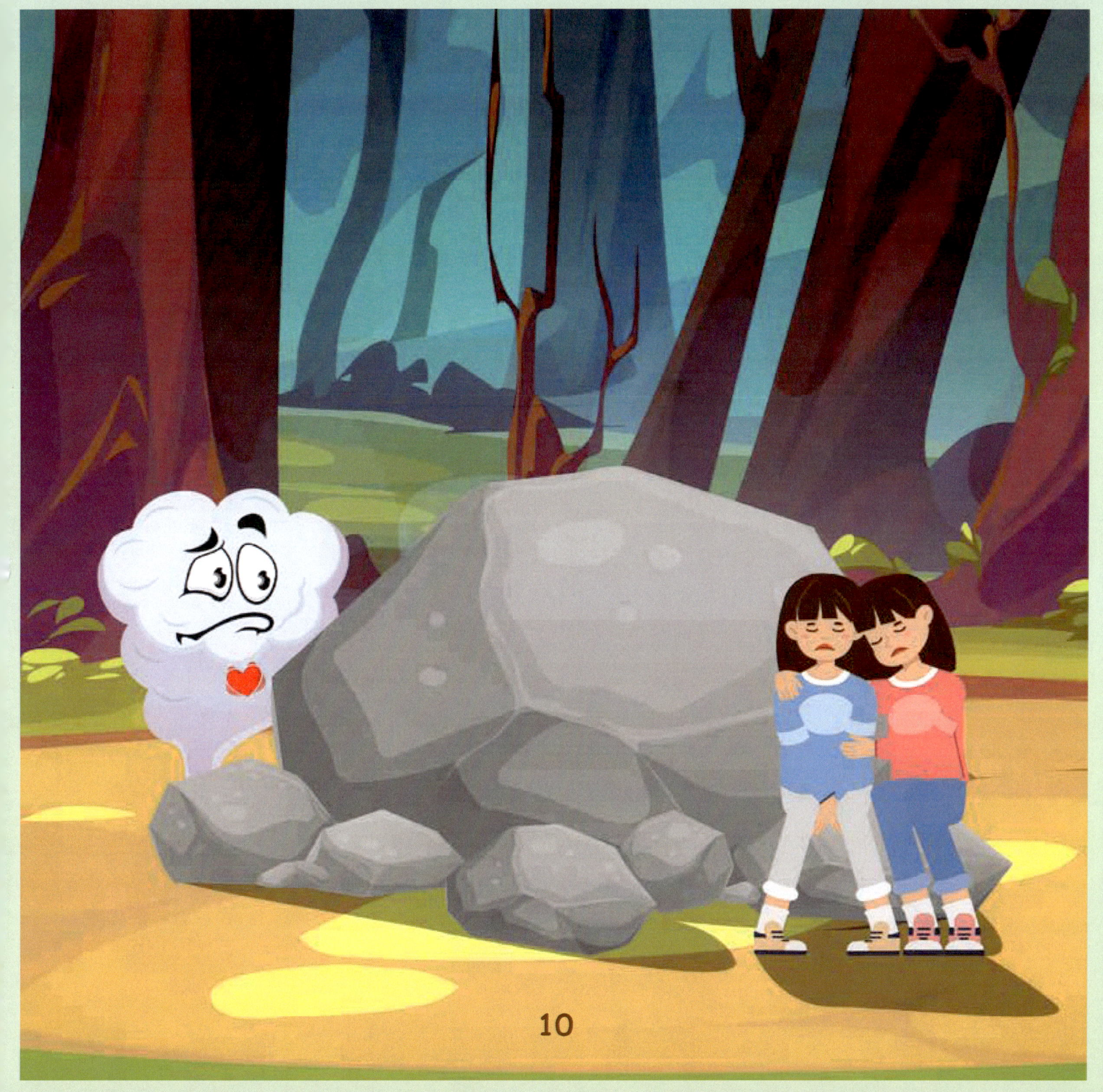

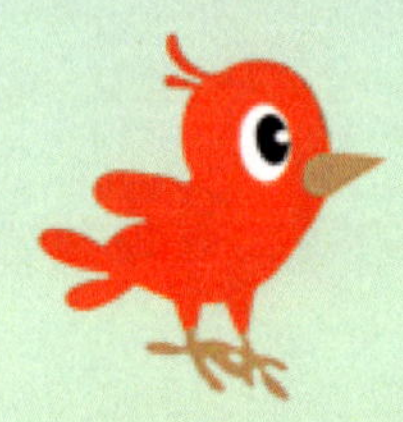

Frank did not want to frighten them and thought that if he was careful, he could help them. Maybe they might even become friends, and this would be the cure for his loneliness.

Frank thought about the best way to meet his potential new friends so he could help them.

Suddenly, he had an idea. He would think himself into becoming a person who was about the same size or maybe just a little bigger than the two girls he saw. That is exactly what he did and that is what he became. Now, he hoped he would become their friend.

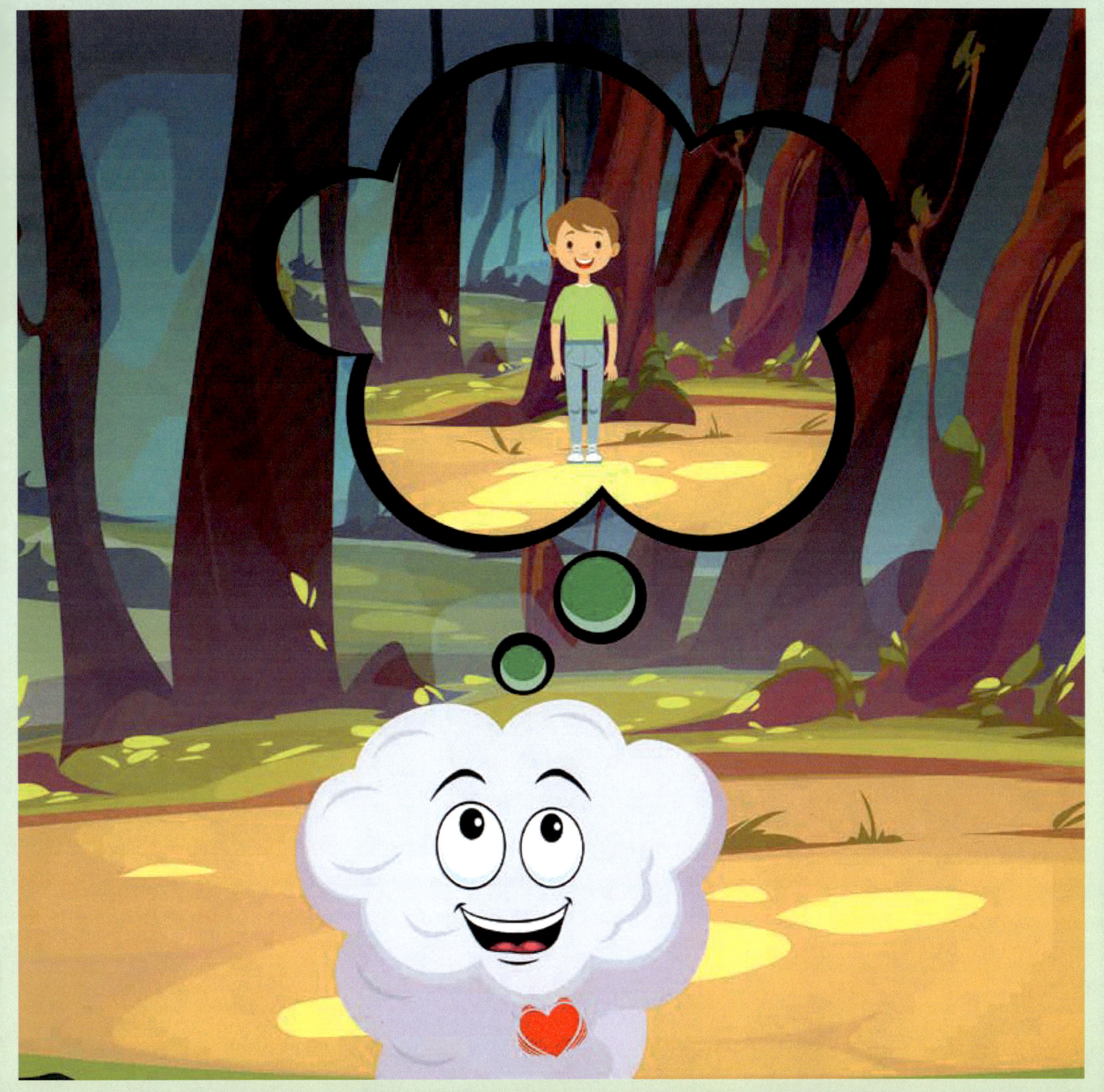

He slowly walked over to them and said in his friendliest and kindest voice, "Hi. I am Frank, and I live in the woods. I can help you if you want me to. Who are you and how did you get here?"

They had seen him coming and held onto each other tighter, but when they heard how friendly his voice sounded, they felt better and said, "Hello, you must be what we have heard about that lives in the woods. But you don't look so scary."

The girls told Frank that they were Emma and Caroline and that they had followed a little red bird into the woods and had gotten lost. They loved birds and worms and all sorts of animals, even those that lived in the woods.

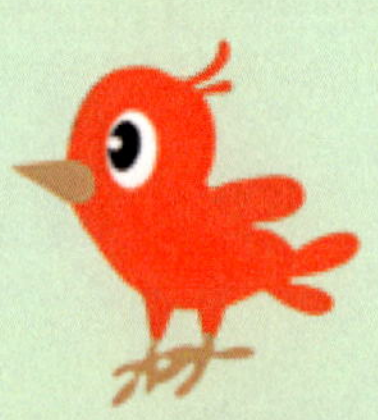

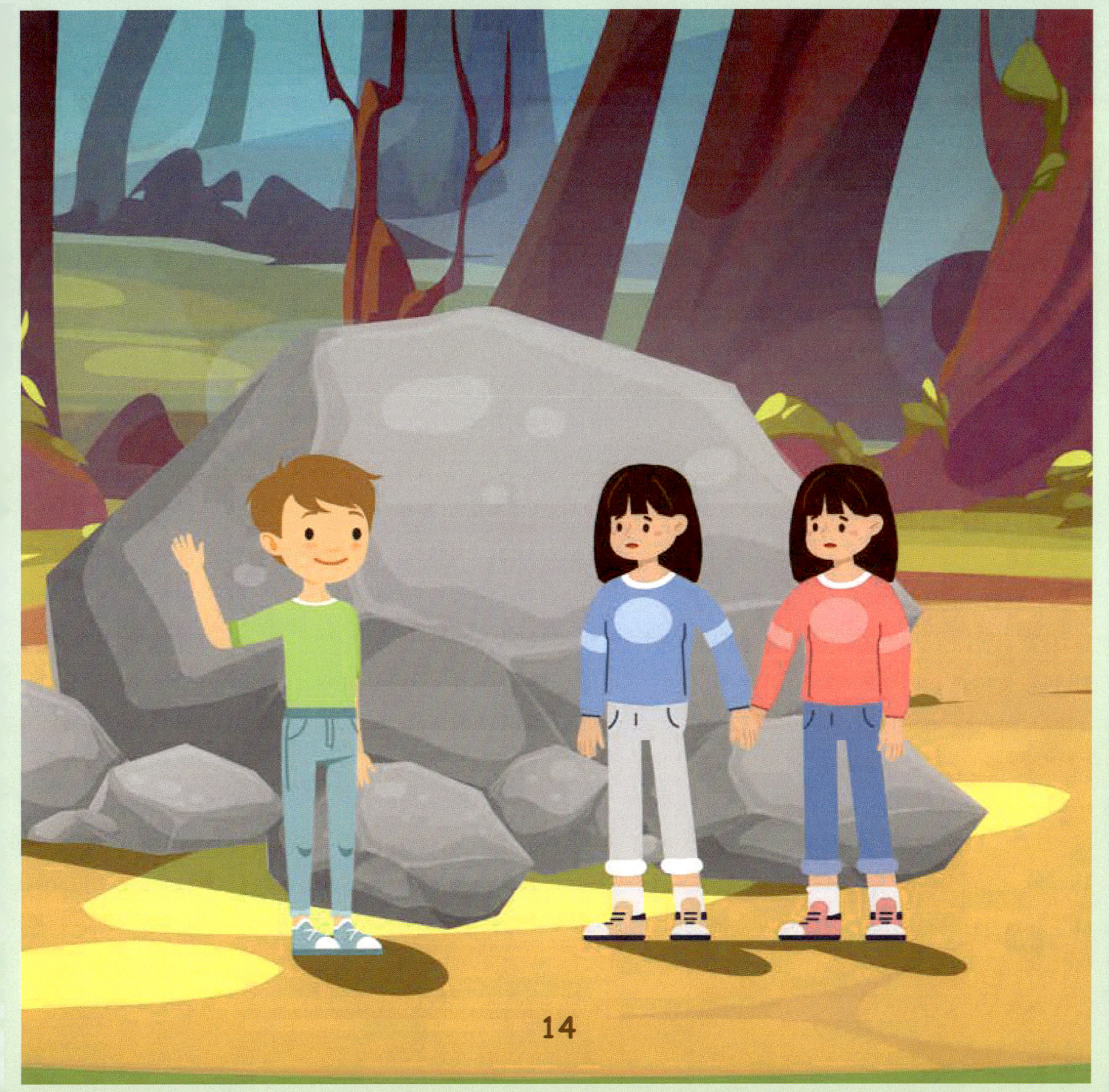

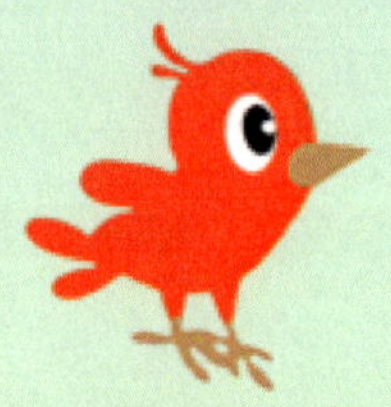

Frank told them that he would show them the way through the woods so they could get home, but he would only go to the edge of the woods. He told them that he had never been outside of the woods and that the woods were his home. He did not feel safe in any place but his home in the woods.

Emma and Caroline felt much better and agreed that they would follow Frank to the edge of the woods and then go home.

Frank, Emma, and Caroline walked together to the edge of the woods and when they got to the last big group of trees, they could see Emma and Caroline's house.

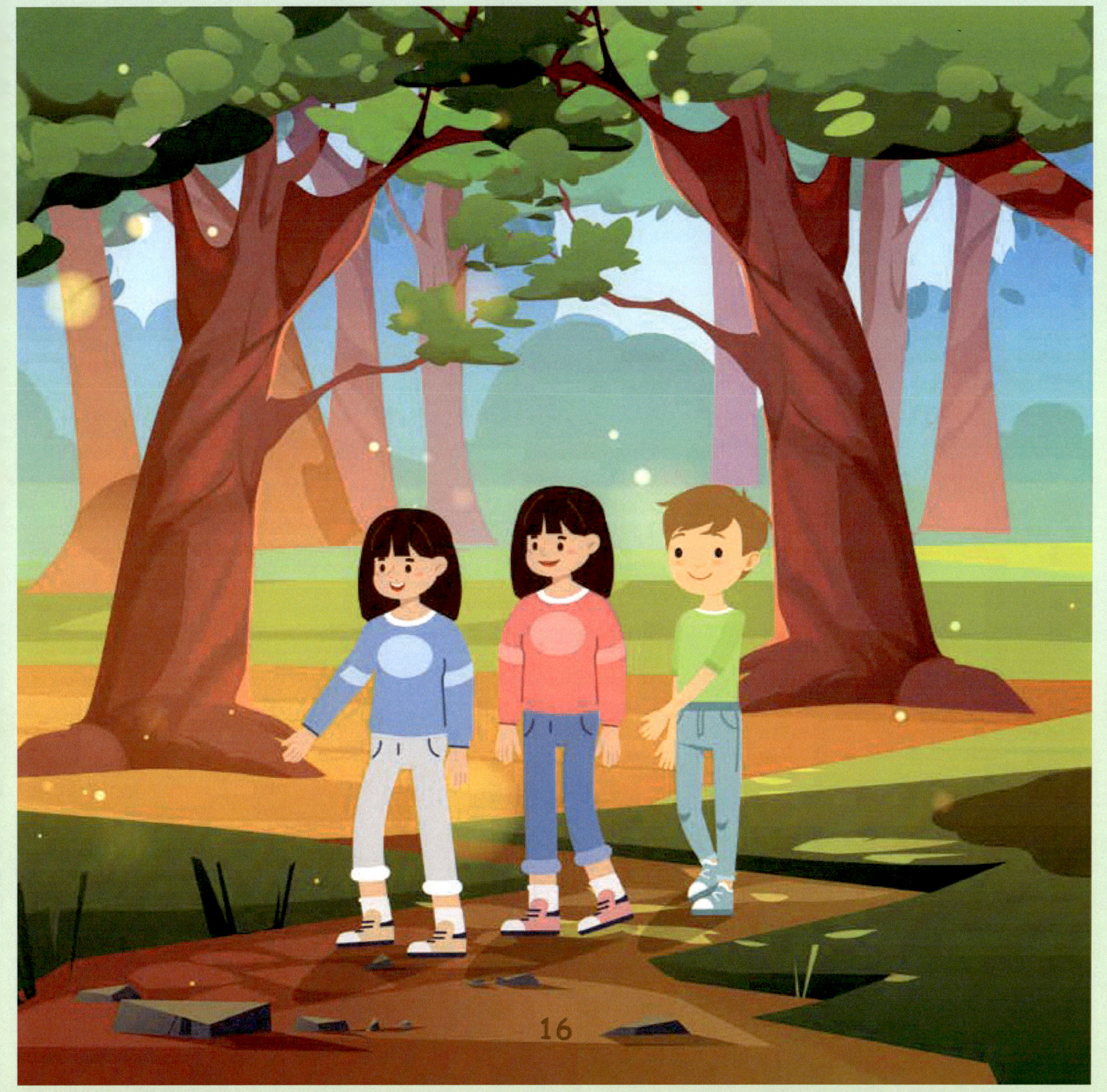

It was time to say goodbye. Frank asked the girls if they could be friends. They said, "Sure, we would love to be your friends."

Frank got a very large smile on his face and promised to see the girls the next time they wanted to go for a walk in the woods.

He said he would see them coming because he knew the woods so well and would hear where they were.

The three new friends said goodbye. As the girls left the forest to go home, Frank watched them to be sure they were safe in their yard. They waved to him one last time and he waved back.

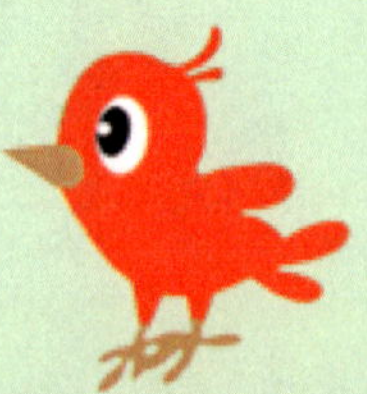

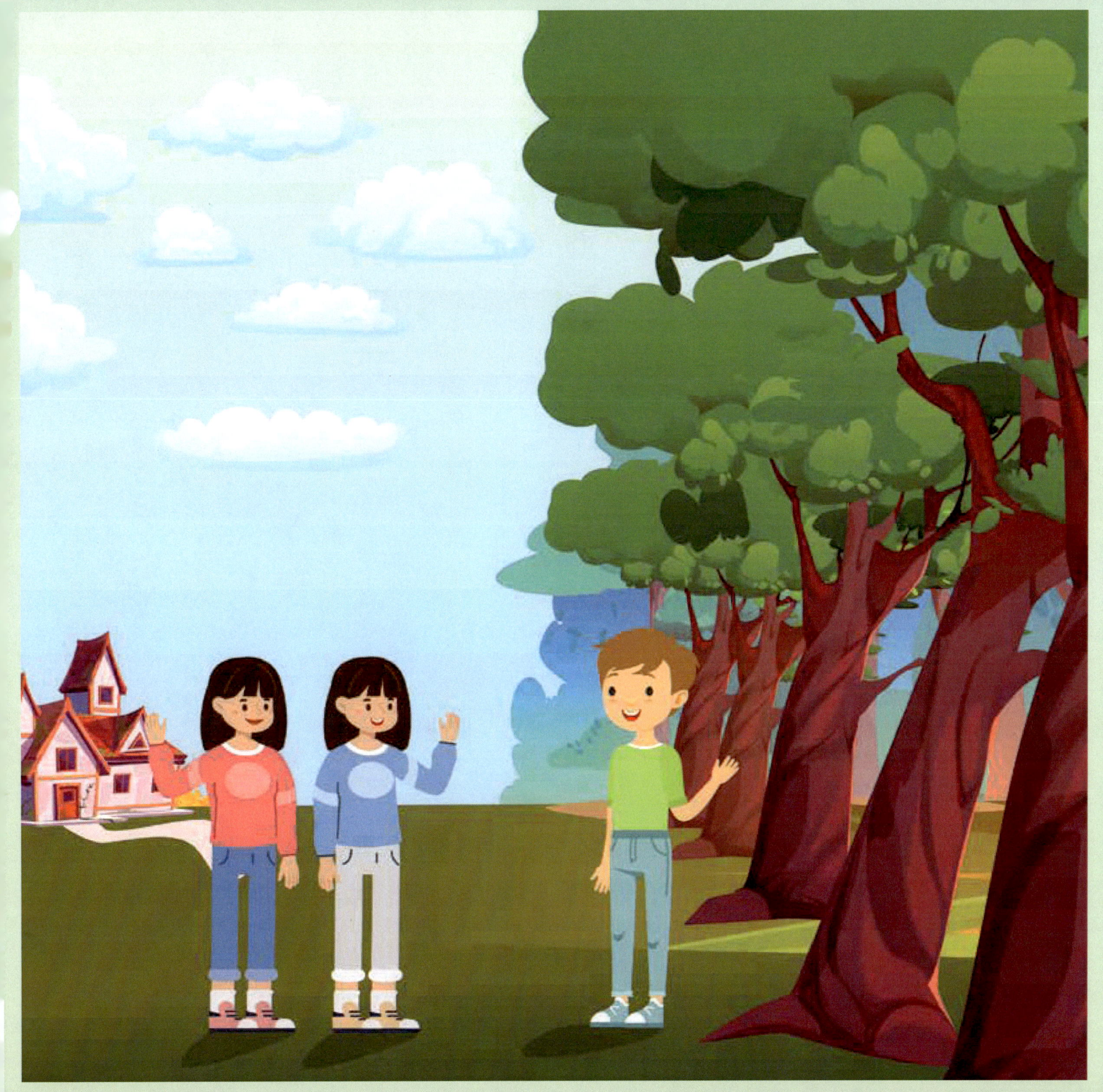

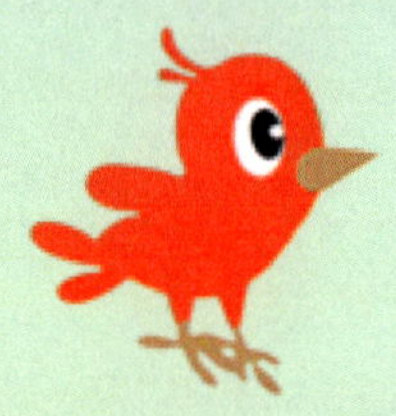

Frank smiled because as the girls were walking back home, he noticed that a little red bird was following them. He wondered if it was the same bird that Emma and Caroline had followed into the woods.

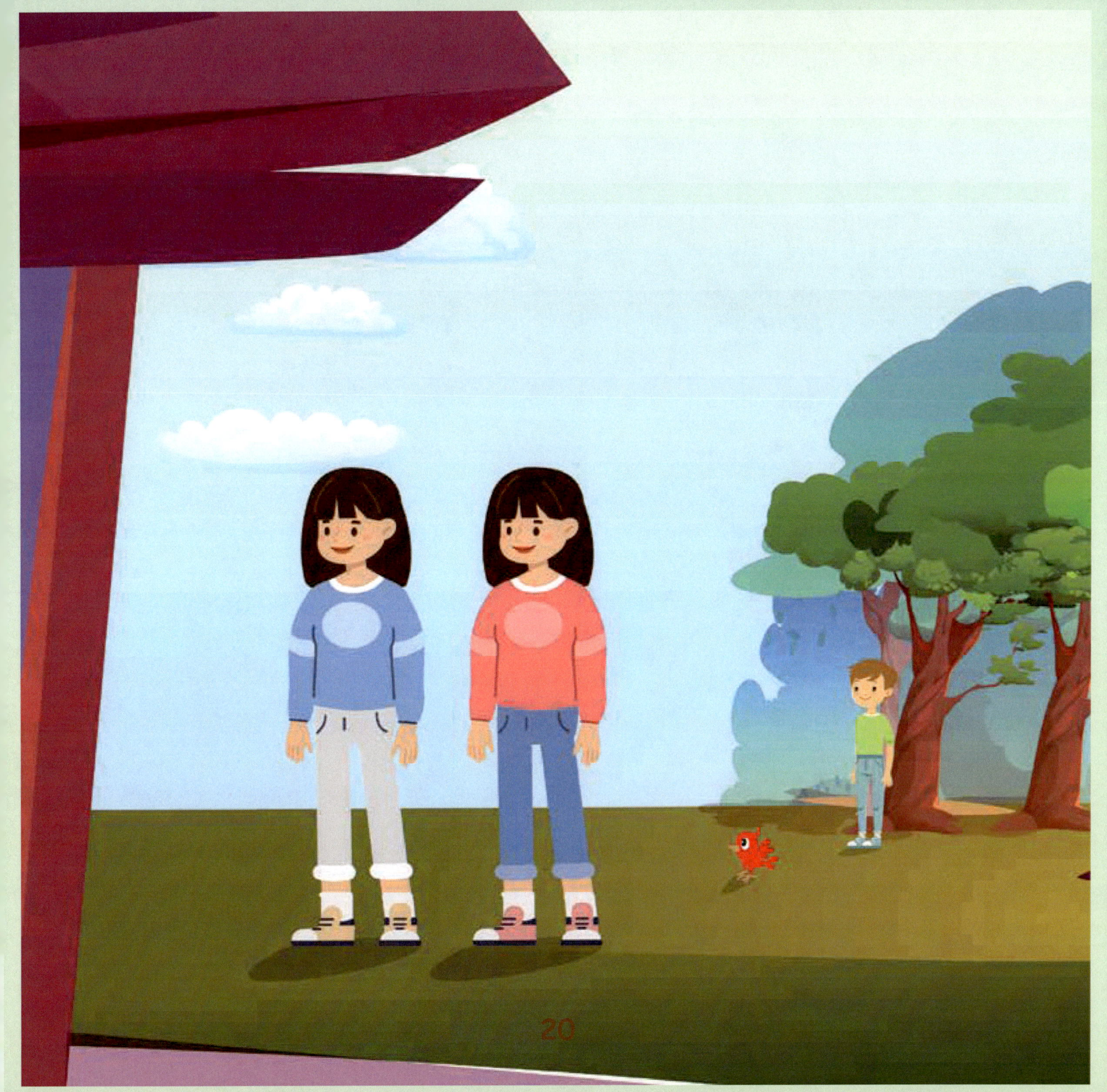

Frank was happy and as he walked deeper and deeper into the woods, towards his home, he thought of Emma and Caroline. They were his new friends, and they were going to have so much fun together. He was so happy thinking about his new friends and not being lonely anymore that he almost forgot to change himself back into being the Frank he knew.

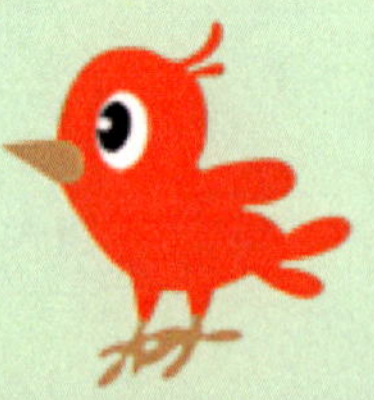

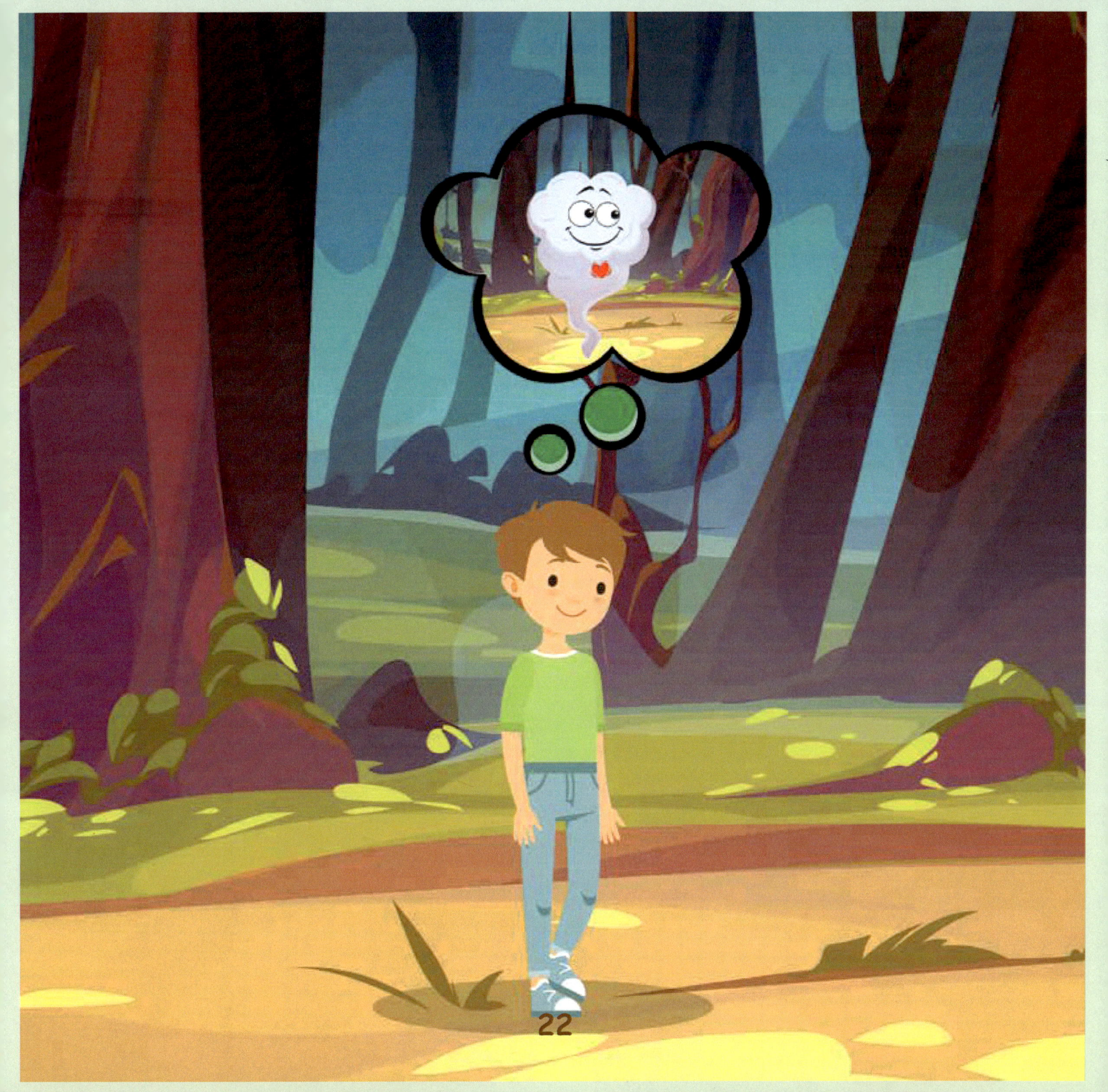

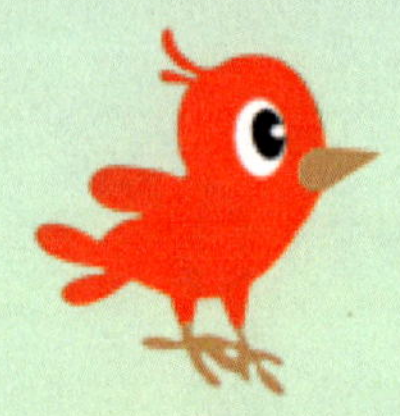

Once he did that, he was again that Frank, the small being with a gigantic heart that only wanted to be friendly and help anyone or anything he could.

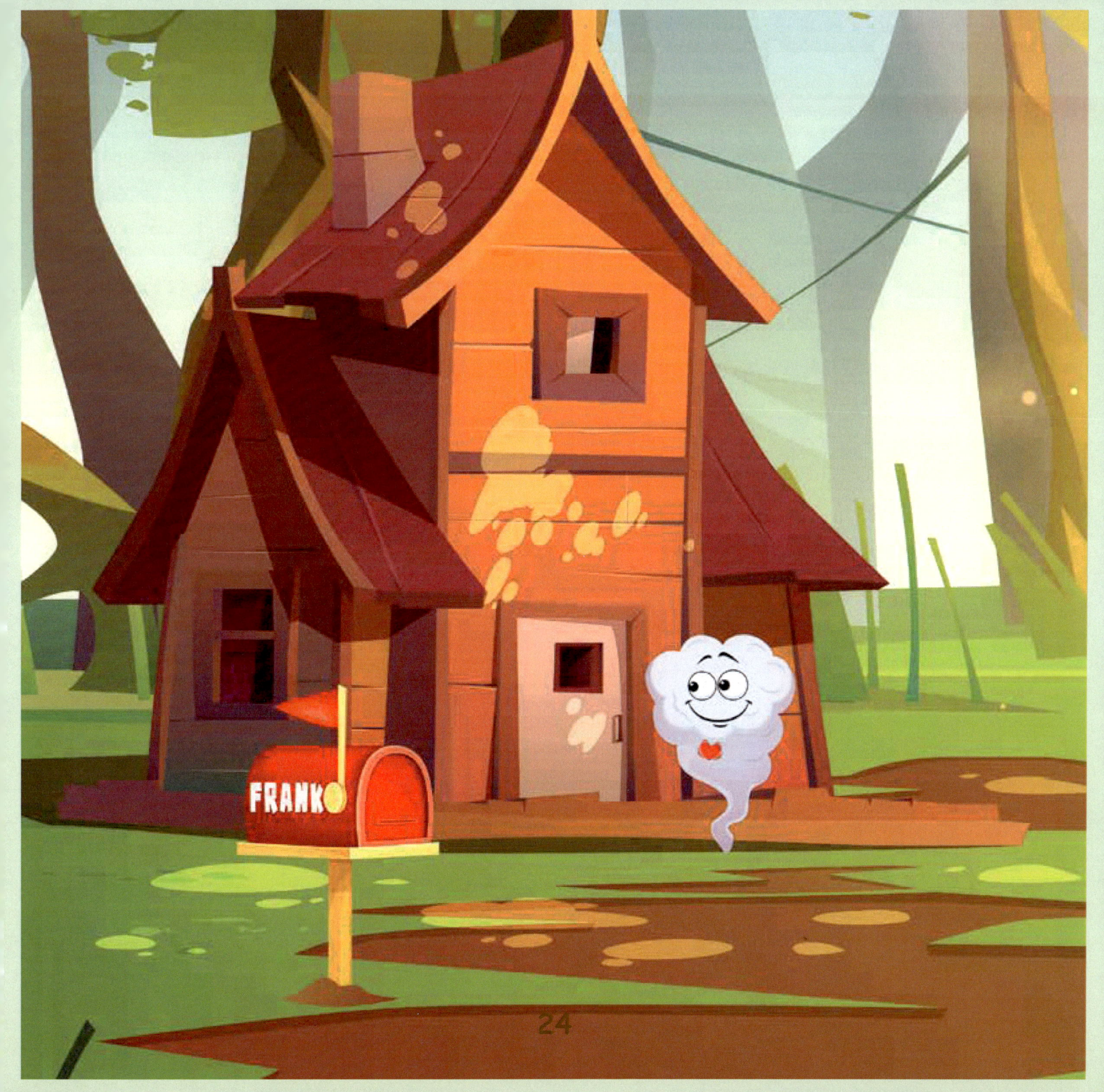
FRANK

Yes, Frank was happy to be at home, but he was also ready to make more new friends and help anyone or anything he could. Who or what would he meet next, and how would he help them? Frank was excited to find out. Are you?

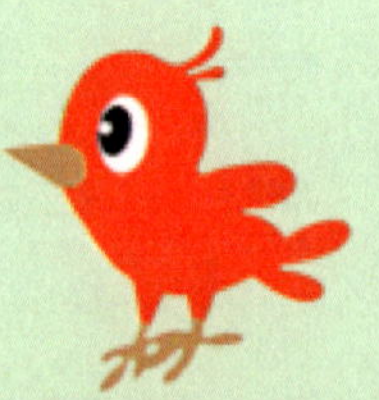

THE END